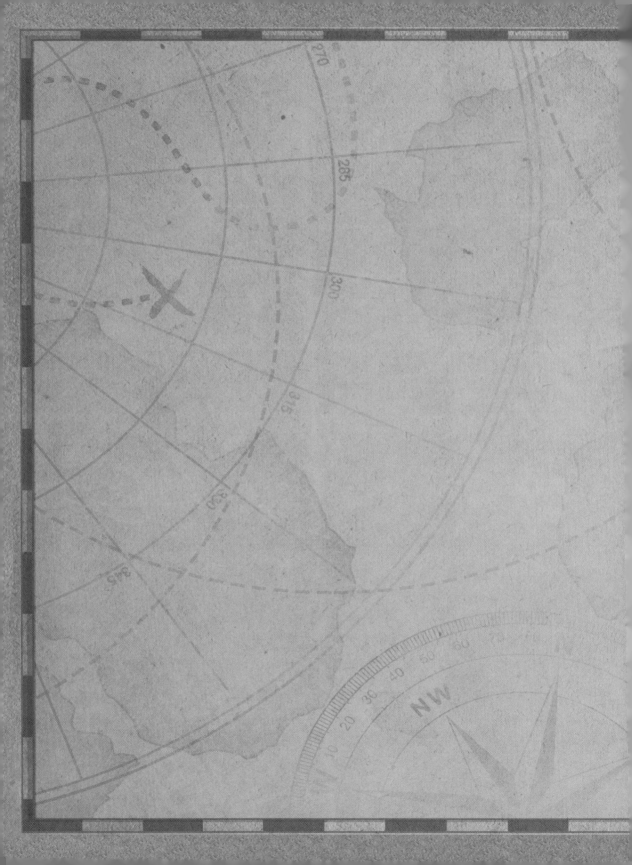

TABLE OF CONTENTS

ADVENTURING 101

SO YOU WANT TO BE A BOLD, BRAVE, BRILLIANT ADVENTURER? YOU WANT TO SWIM IN STACKS OF GOLD LIKE SCROOGE McDUCK, AMASSED FROM TREASURES EXCAVATED ON EXCITING ESCAPADES? YOU WANT TO UNLOCK DOORS, SCALE WALLS AND CLIMB THE HIGHEST MOUNTAINS OR DESCEND INTO THE DARKEST DEPTHS ON A QUEST FOR FUN WHILE STILL MAKING IT HOME IN TIME FOR DINNER? THEN THIS IS THE GUIDE FOR YOU! BUT BEFORE YOU SET OUT AND BECOME THE NEXT LEWIS AND CLARK OR AMELIA EARHART, YOU'VE GOT TO GET A FEW BASICS DOWN FIRST.

BE SAFE

WHEN YOU'RE OUT EXPLORING, THE MOST IMPORTANT THING YOU CAN BE IS SAFE! AFTER ALL, YOU WON'T BE ABLE TO GO ON MORE ADVENTURES IF YOU'RE LAID UP IN BED.

1. ALWAYS BRING A BUDDY (OR THREE!)

Whether you're going on a hike, kayaking in a lake or searching for the Jewel of Atlantis, you should bring your adventuring friends along with you! You and your friends can take turns being lookouts, search areas together quickly and, most importantly, call each other—or an adult—for help if you need it.

2. DON'T EXPLORE UNFAMILIAR PLACES

It's not a good idea to go into a cave without a guide, or go searching through Ithaquack's Temple of Heroes without directions! Never put yourself in a situation where you could get lost and not be able to find your way back.

3. ASK PERMISSION

Just because you're an adventurer doesn't mean you get to make your own rules. Always call your parent or guardian and tell them where you are, and don't bother lying— as Webby learned when she lied to her grandmother about going to Atlantis, they always know!

GET FIT

IF YOU'RE GOING TO
BE AN ADVENTURER,
YOU NEED TO BE IN
TIP-TOP CONDITION.
CLIMBING MOUNTAINS,
STOPPING GIANT
ROBOTS AND SPENDING
ALL DAY LOOKING FOR
LOST RELICS ISN'T A
WALK IN THE PARK—
IT'S MORE LIKE
A MARATHON!

1. BUILD UP YOUR ENDURANCE

How long can you run? You better hope it's for more time than a
Terra-firmian! (Though actually, Terra-firmians are pretty nice.)
Practice your long-distance running—just in case you need it.
Start by seeing how long you can run before you get tired, and
try to push yourself a little longer or farther each day.

2. GET STRONGER

You're going to need lots of strength to pull yourself up the side of a mountain, and even more to carry all your treasure home afterward! Push-ups are a great way to build up arm strength. Can you do 10 of them without stopping? Yeah? How about 25? Set a goal for yourself and make it happen!

3. BE FLEXIBLE

Sometimes being able to reach just a tiny bit farther makes the difference when you're trying to escape a perilous situation or grab a mysterious glowing orb. Practice by touching your toes (or flippers), and if that's too easy, tuck your chin to your chest and try again.

BE SMART

A LITTLE BIT OF PLANNING GOES A LONG WAY! RESEARCH IS OFTEN THE MOST CRUCIAL PART OF AN ADVENTURE—AND BESIDES, PLANNING IS FUN!

WE NEED A PLAN!

1. LEARN EVERYTHING YOU CAN ABOUT YOUR MISSION

Whether you're searching for the Spear of Selene or planning to climb Mt. Neverrest, it's best to know everything you can about your destination! Search online, go to your local library and look for reference books or ask questions of a more seasoned adventurer.

t Neverrest Summit: rnnlexing peaks known to man.

2. CHECK THE WEATHER

If it's going to snow, it might not be a great day to go exploring by the beach. But if it's snowing on the Drake Barrier Reef, It's the perfect time to visit Atlantis!

3. BE AWARE OF YOUR SURROUNDINGS

Always pay attention to what's going on around you. Whether it's a root that you could have tripped over or Pixiu the gold-hunting dragon trying to steal your fortune, there's danger at every turn when you're out adventuring. That's why it's important to keep your eyes peeled at all times.

ADVENTURING BASICS

BEFORE YOU PLAN A TRIP TO THE GOLDEN LAGOON OF WHITE AGONY PLAINS OR FIND YOURSELF BATTLING A MONEY SHARK, YOU SHOULD BRUSH UP ON THE BASICS OF ADVENTURING! IN THIS SECTION, DISCOVER THE BASICS OF TYING KNOTS, DOCUMENTING YOUR ADVENTURES, LEARNING ABOUT OTHER FAMOUS EXPLORERS AND MUCH MORE!

PACK YOUR ADVENTURE BAG

SOMETIMES ADVENTURE CAN'T WAIT FOR YOU TO GRAB YOUR THINGS, WHICH IS WHY YOU SHOULD HAVE A PACKED BAG READY TO GO AT ANY TIME!* MAKE SURE NOT TO STOW AWAY ANYTHING THAT MIGHT ROT—THAT MEANS NO EGGS. AND UNLIKE DONALD, TRY NOT TO OVERPACK!

THINGS TO INCLUDE

 • WATER CONTAINERS

• BATTERIES • COMPASS • GRANOLA BARS/NUTS

• A CHANGE OF CLOTHES
(OR AT LEAST UNDERWEAR!)

• FLASHLIGHT • BANDAGES

• BABY WIPES
(SO YOU CAN KEEP CLEAN!)

• BINOCULARS

* JUST DON'T SET OFF WITHOUT TELLING AN ADULT WHERE YOU'RE GOING!

THE PERFECT CLUBHOUSE

A CLUBHOUSE IS LIKE YOUR HOME AWAY FROM HOME. PICK A PLACE THAT'S SECLUDED, FILL IT WITH AWESOME STUFF AND INVITE OVER SOME FELLOW ADVENTURERS—IT'S THE PERFECT PLACE TO PLAN YOUR NEXT EXPEDITION!

(OR IF YOU'RE FLINTHEART GLOMGOLD, TO PLAN HOW TO FOIL SCROOGE.)

CLUBHOUSE ESSENTIALS

- THIS ADVENTURE GUIDE

- NIGHT-VISION GOGGLES

- FIRST AID KIT

- PILLOWS AND BLANKETS, FOR LOUNGING

- SNACKS

- MAPS
- BOARD GAMES
- HISTORY BOOKS **IF YOU ARE WEBBY, THAT IS!**

POTENTIAL CLUBHOUSE SPOTS

BOATHOUSE

TREEHOUSE

BASEMENT OR GARAGE

BACKYARD TENT

TIE BASIC KNOTS

HUEY SHOWED THE BEAGLE BOYS JUST HOW USEFUL KNOT TYING CAN BE, WHETHER FOR MAKING A SNARE OR TYING UP SOME JUNK YARD STEW!

CLOVE HITCH

ALSO KNOWN AS A DOUBLE HITCH, THE CLOVE HITCH IS A QUICK, TEMPORARY KNOT COMMONLY USED FOR SECURING A LINE ON A POST.

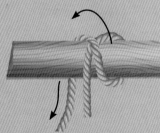

TO MAKE THIS KNOT

1. PASS THE END OF THE ROPE AROUND A POST.

2. BRING THE ROPE AROUND AND CROSS OVER.

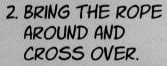

3. BRING THE ROPE BEHIND AND TO THE LEFT OF THE OTHER END.

4. TUCK UNDER. THIS IS A HALF HITCH.

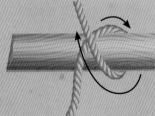

5. PULL ENDS TO TIGHTEN AROUND POST.

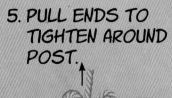

6. FINISHED KNOT.

TIMBER HITCH

THE TIMBER HITCH IS USEFUL FOR DRAGGING LOGS AND EASILY COMES LOOSE WHEN YOU STOP PULLING ON IT.

TO MAKE THIS KNOT

1. PLACE ROPE BEHIND THE POST OR LOG.

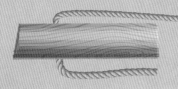

2. PASS BOTTOM END OVER THE POST, UNDER THE TOP END THEN OVER THE TOP END.

3. TUCK THE SAME END UNDER ITSELF AGAINST THE POST.

4. WRAP THE END AROUND THAT CROSS POINT TWO MORE TIMES.

5. PULL ENDS TO TIGHTEN AROUND POST.

6. FINISHED KNOT.

DON'T GET TOO TIED UP!

UNTIE STUBBORN KNOTS

SOMETIMES, ALL YOU WANT IS TO UNTIE A KNOT—
ESPECIALLY IF IT'S ANYTHING LIKE THE ONE
WEBBY USED TO TRAP HUEY, DEWEY AND LOUIE!

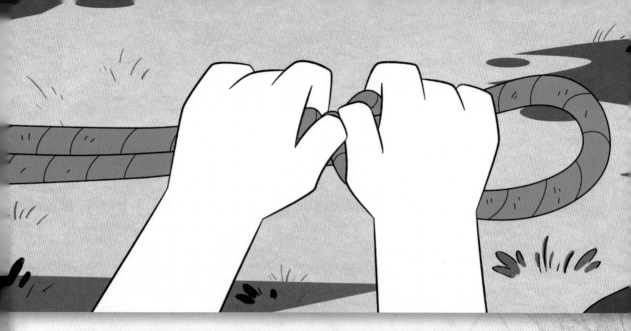

If you need to untie a super tight knot, it can be pretty difficult—unless you know this trick! It works on almost any knot.

All you have to do is twist the loose end of the knot until it becomes tight and stiff, and then push it through the rest of the knot!

For knots where there isn't a loose end, you can also try using something smaller and with a better grip than your fingers, like tweezers.

If all else fails, just use scissors or a knife (with an adult's help). We don't recommend Webby's method of using your teeth!

DOCUMENT YOUR ADVENTURES

EVERY GOOD ADVENTURER MAKES SURE TO RECORD THEIR EXPERIENCES, INCLUDING WHERE THEY WENT, WHAT THEY FOUND AND HOW THEY DID IT. WEBBY EVEN COVERS HER JOURNAL IN GLITTER, SO SHE CAN SEE IF ANYONE'S BEEN SNOOPING THROUGH HER RECORDS!

THERE ARE THREE REASONS FOR DOCUMENTING ADVENTURES

1. It's important to leave behind a record of your discoveries and experiences for other adventurers and historians to learn from.

2. Keeping a journal of your experiences ensures you don't forget them, or what they taught you. It's important to remember the past!

3. Things you discover today might be of value during future adventures. For example, if you find half a map showing the way to the Golden Lagoon of White Agony Plains, it will come in handy if you ever meet someone with the other half!

THERE ARE A FEW BASIC TOOLS YOU'LL NEED IN ORDER TO DOCUMENT YOUR ADVENTURES ACCURATELY

- A SMALL NOTEPAD OR JOURNAL

- A FRESH PEN

- A SHARP PENCIL

- RUBBING PAPER (A THIN SHEET OF PARCHMENT PAPER FROM YOUR KITCHEN WILL DO)

- A THICK BLACK CRAYON WITH THE PAPER WRAPPING REMOVED

- A SMALL FLASHLIGHT

THE SECRET FILES OF WEBIGAIL VANDERQUACK

KNOWLEDGE IS THE GREATEST WEAPON OF ALL!

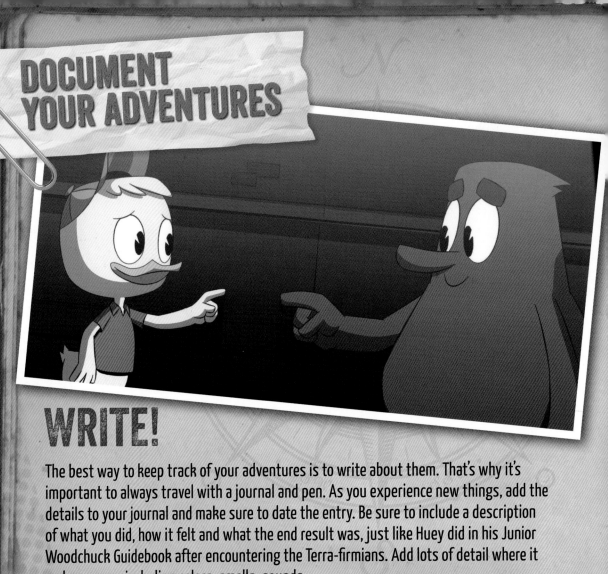

WRITE!

The best way to keep track of your adventures is to write about them. That's why it's important to always travel with a journal and pen. As you experience new things, add the details to your journal and make sure to date the entry. Be sure to include a description of what you did, how it felt and what the end result was, just like Huey did in his Junior Woodchuck Guidebook after encountering the Terra-firmians. Add lots of detail where it makes sense, including colors, smells, sounds and so on—whatever makes the experience memorable to you and a fun read for anyone else you'd like to share the experience with.

AND LOGGED IT!
NO LONGER UNKNOWN.
THEY EXIST.
SCIENCE FACT!

SKETCH!

Another great way to record your experiences is through sketching. If you discover the Medusa Gauntlet, you definitely shouldn't touch it, but you can sketch it! Draw the image in your journal with a pencil and provide a description of your experience with the subject next to it. It's like creating an illustrated guide to your own story!

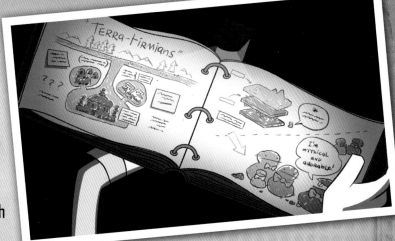

RECORD!

Finally, use rubbing paper anytime you come across raised letters, numbers or symbols (sometimes referred to as glyphs) that you want to copy. This is an especially good idea if you're visiting somewhere like the Lost Pyramids of Toth-Ra!

Place the rubbing paper on top of the glyphs and spread it out nice and flat. Then take your black crayon and rub it lengthwise across the surface of the paper. The edges of the glyphs will show up on the topside of the material, creating an impressive copy of the details beneath. Artifacts like this are helpful tools for remembering—and sharing—the details of past adventures.

IN ALL OF THESE CASES, YOU'LL WANT TO HAVE A SMALL FLASHLIGHT ON HAND SO THAT YOU CAN DRAFT A NEW ENTRY WHEN NEEDED. IT'S TOUGH TO DRAW OR WRITE WHEN THE LIGHT IS LOW AND YOU HAVEN'T GOT TIME TO WAIT FOR BETTER CONDITIONS.

FIRST AID

KNOWING SOME BASIC FIRST AID IS VITAL TO BECOMING A RESPONSIBLE ADVENTURER! (NOTE: KNOWING FIRST AID ISN'T AN EXCUSE FOR DANGEROUS BEHAVIOR!)

THE THREE C'S

BEFORE ANY HELP CAN BE ADMINISTERED, YOU SHOULD ALWAYS KEEP IN MIND THE THREE C'S.

CHECK THE SURROUNDINGS

Make sure there is no immediate danger. What hurt the victim could easily hurt you too, and you're no help if you get injured as well.

CALL FOR HELP

If it's a major injury, it's best to get help as soon as possible. Call an adult, or dial 911 if it's clear the person needs a doctor.

CARE FOR THE VICTIM

Keeping the victim calm until help can be administered is very important. Be calm and collected and make sure the victim knows help is on the way.

TREATING MINOR CUTS, SCRAPES AND ABRASIONS

WASH YOUR HANDS

Unclean hands could infect the wound, so make sure to wash thoroughly before anything is done. You definitely don't want an infection!

CLEAN THE AREA AROUND THE WOUND

First, keep the cut under a steady stream of warm water. While that is happening, begin washing the outer area with soap, but make sure not to get any soap in the wound itself.

APPLY ANTIBIOTICS

If you have an antibiotic gel or ointment, apply it gently to the cut.

WHETHER YOU'RE AS UNLUCKY AS DONALD DUCK OR AS FORTUNATE AS GLADSTONE GANDER, IT PAYS TO KNOW FIRST AID!

BANDAGE THE WOUND

Take a bandage or a piece of medical gauze and gently wrap it around the cut, securing with medical tape if necessary.

FAMOUS ADVENTURERS AND EXPLORERS

SCROOGE McDUCK ISN'T THE ONLY TRAVELER WITH A THIRST FOR THE UNKNOWN! CHECK OUT THESE OTHER ADVENTURERS AND THEIR INCREDIBLE EXPLOITS.

JACQUES COUSTEAU

Scuba divers everywhere can thank Jacques Cousteau for his scuba equipment! Known for co-inventing the Aqua-Lung, the first piece of equipment that enabled people to go scuba diving, "Captain" Cousteau is remembered for all of his underwater adventures. In 1948, he famously went on an expedition to find the sunken Roman ship *Mahdia*. Twenty years later, Cousteau made a television series so people around the world could watch him go on his oceanic expeditions.

Duck Data:
Scuba is actually an acronym! It stands for "Self Contained Underwater Breathing Apparatus."

AMELIA EARHART

A fearless flyer, Amelia Earhart could have taught Launchpad a thing or two about flying a plane. She was the first woman to fly solo across the Atlantic Ocean and was the first person to fly solo from Hawaii to the U.S. mainland. Her final flight remains a mystery: In her 1937 attempt to fly around the world, she disappeared somewhere over the Pacific. Neither Earhart nor her plane have ever been found.

NEIL ARMSTRONG

On July 20, 1969, Neil Armstrong became the first person to walk on the moon—a place that hasn't even been visited by Scrooge McDuck (at least, not yet). He and fellow astronaut Buzz Aldrin stayed on the moon for 21 hours. Because there isn't any wind on the moon, their footprints are still there!

ISABELLA BIRD

From around 1870 to 1900, Englishwoman Isabella Bird traveled by herself all over the world—something very few women did at that time! She climbed an active volcano in Hawaii, rode alone through a blizzard in the Rocky Mountains, traveled to Japan, Hong Kong, Singapore, Malay Peninsula, India and more. (We bet she would have gotten along well with Mrs. Beakley.) She wrote many books about her travels, and in 1890 she received the honor of becoming the first female Fellow of the U.K.'s Royal Geographical Society.

ADVENTURING OUTDOORS

GET READY TO EXPERIENCE
ALL THE WONDERS OF NATURE!
LEARN HOW TO MAKE SNOW GOGGLES
(PERFECT FOR CLIMBING MT. NEVERREST),
HOW TO PAN FOR GOLD (IT'S NEVER TOO
EARLY TO MAKE YOUR OWN MONEY BIN),
READ TOPOGRAPHIC MAPS
AND A WHOLE LOT MORE!

HOW TO FIND TRUE NORTH

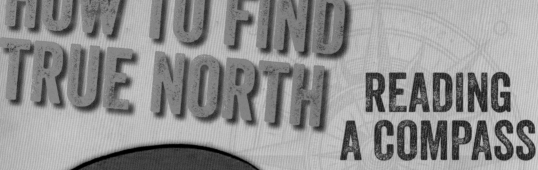

READING A COMPASS

A COMPASS IS ALWAYS A HANDY TOOL, WHETHER YOU'RE SETTING OUT FOR FUNSO'S FUN ZONE OR FLYING IN THE SUNCHASER! AS LONG AS YOU KNOW THE DIRECTION YOU NEED TO GO, YOUR COMPASS WILL POINT YOU THERE.

USING YOUR COMPASS

Hold your compass out in front of you. The magnetized part of the compass, called a needle, will always point north, no matter which way you hold it. Turn the compass until the tip of the needle (usually marked with an N) aligns with the N at the top of your compass, and now you can see which ways are north, east, west and south!

FINDING YOUR WAY WITHOUT A COMPASS

IF YOU'RE OUT EXPLORING, A COMPASS IS A MUST-HAVE. BUT WHAT DO YOU DO IF YOUR PILOT'S COMPASS IS ACTUALLY A DECAL?

WE ARE BEYOND LOST, AND... IS THIS COMPASS A STICKER?!

CHECK THE SUN

No matter where you are, be it Duckburg or Ithaquack, the sun rises in the east and sets in the west. If it's morning or evening, you should be able to figure out which direction north is based on the position of the sun. But if it's the middle of the day, it can be tough to determine which direction the sun is moving, so you may want to use the Shadow Method.

SOUTH

NORTH!

THE SHADOW METHOD

Find a spot on the ground with plenty of direct sunlight. Place a stick upright in the ground, and use a rock or other object to mark the tip of its shadow. Wait 15 to 20 minutes, and mark where the tip of the shadow has moved. The shadow will have moved from west to east. If you stand between the shadows with the first mark on your left, you are facing north.

HOW TO READ A TOPOGRAPHIC MAP

EVERY YOUNG ADVENTURER SHOULD KNOW HOW TO READ A TOPOGRAPHIC MAP. THEY PROVIDE INFORMATION THAT CAN MAKE YOUR EXPLORATIONS MUCH EASIER AND HELP KEEP YOU FROM GETTING LOST (OR, IF YOU'RE GLOMGOLD, HELP YOU TRACK DOWN WHERE YOUR NEMESIS IS).

A topographic map may look a little odd the first time you see one, but all of the wavy circular lines and patterns have a very specific purpose—they measure the shape and features of the Earth's surface.

When you're reading a topographic map, find the point on the map where you are and compare it to the landmarks around you. Once you've oriented yourself to the map, you can follow or cross the contour lines, so long as you keep the landmarks and elevation around you oriented to the map. Then you're that much closer to finding the Jewel of Atlantis!

HOW TO READ A TOPOGRAPHIC MAP

HERE ARE A FEW GUIDELINES THAT WILL HELP EXPLAIN EXACTLY WHAT ALL THOSE LINES MEAN

- The lines on a topographic map are called contour lines.

- Each contour line represents the same elevation at any point on the line, so if a line is marked as representing an elevation of 800 meters, any point on that line will also be at 800 meters.

- Contour lines separate uphill from downhill, so the inside of a contour line represents an increase in elevation, while the outside of a contour line represents a decrease.

- The innermost circle represents the highest point of land in that area of the map—like the top of a hill, or even a mountain! As you move outside of each circle, the elevation decreases until you arrive at the lowest point of elevation in the area, such as the bottom of a valley.

- Contour lines are close together in steep terrain, because the elevation is changing quickly in this area on the map.

- Contour lines are far apart in areas where elevation does not change often, such as along a wide river bed or open field.

- Contour lines never touch each other, nor do they cross. The only exception to this rule is when you're looking at a vertical cliff wall or cave.

119

100

64

50

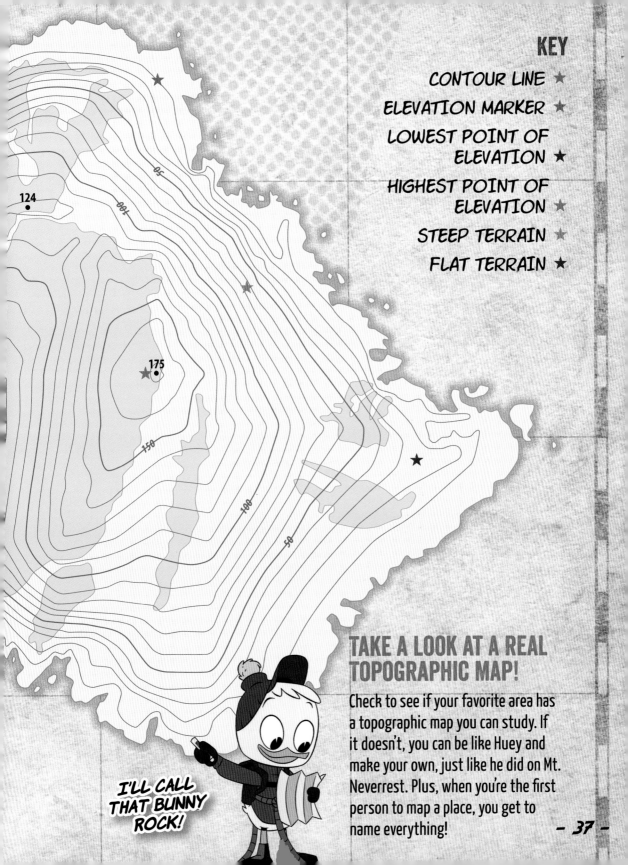

KEY

CONTOUR LINE ★
ELEVATION MARKER ★
LOWEST POINT OF ELEVATION ★
HIGHEST POINT OF ELEVATION ★
STEEP TERRAIN ★
FLAT TERRAIN ★

TAKE A LOOK AT A REAL TOPOGRAPHIC MAP!

Check to see if your favorite area has a topographic map you can study. If it doesn't, you can be like Huey and make your own, just like he did on Mt. Neverrest. Plus, when you're the first person to map a place, you get to name everything!

I'LL CALL THAT BUNNY ROCK!

MAKE YOUR OWN SNOW GOGGLES

SOMETIMES YOU MAY FIND YOURSELF IN THE FROZEN NORTH, WHERE BRIGHT WHITE SNOW COVERS EVERYTHING FOR MONTHS. THE GLARE OF THE SUN REFLECTED OFF OF THIS SNOW CAN BE HARMFUL TO YOUR EYES OVER TIME. THINK OF IT LIKE GETTING A SUNBURN, ONLY RIGHT ON YOUR EYEBALLS. YIKES!

Smart adventurers know that in snowy conditions, it's just as important to protect your eyes as it is to wear warm boots and gloves. Sunglasses are great for cutting down the sun's glare, but if you find yourself in an emergency situation where you don't have any, don't be like Launchpad and get taken in by a snake oil salesman—they'll also try to sell you a bunch of supplies you don't need to protect you from the deadly ravages of ice fever. (Note: Ice fever is not real.) Instead, make your own Inuit-style snow goggles!

READY TO WEAR, SHUT OUT THE GLARE

1. Find a piece of cardboard that's at least as wide as your face. A thin piece is best, as it will be easier to wear and see through, but any cardboard will do.

2. Cut it into the rectangular shape of a mask. Hold the mask up to your face and put your fingers where you know your eyes are in relation to the mask.

3. Have a friend mark these points on the mask with a pen, then cut two horizontal lines across each point, about an inch and a half wide in both places. Make sure the horizontal cuts are not so big that a lot of bright light gets through, but still big enough that you can see through them (otherwise wearing the goggles isn't going to be so helpful). Also be sure to cut a slot for your nose to poke through.

4. Punch a small hole about an inch or so from each end of the mask. Thread a string, a shoelace or even a rubber band through these holes and put the mask on your face. Tie the ends together. Make sure the string isn't so tight you can't remove the mask easily, but don't make it so loose that the mask doesn't sit firmly on your face when you're wearing it. That's critical to keeping out any unwanted glare. It might take some trial and error to figure out exactly where to tie the knot—and you'll have to be careful not to tear the cardboard while you do it—but it's worth the effort!

ONCE YOUR SNOW GOGGLES ARE COMPLETE, YOUR EYES WILL BE SAFE FROM THE LANDSCAPE'S BLINDING LIGHT.

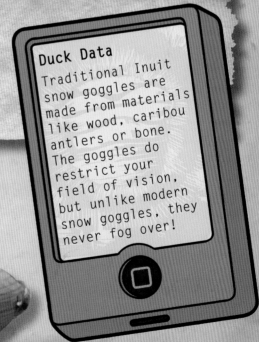

Duck Data
Traditional Inuit snow goggles are made from materials like wood, caribou antlers or bone. The goggles do restrict your field of vision, but unlike modern snow goggles, they never fog over!

LOOK UNDERWATER

YOU DON'T ALWAYS HAVE TO HOP IN A SUBMARINE AND VENTURE ALL THE WAY TO ATLANTIS TO SEE WHAT'S HAPPENING UNDERWATER! CHECKING OUT SHALLOW BODIES OF WATER CAN YIELD GREAT TREASURES, TOO!

BUILD AN UNDERWATER VIEWER

It's actually quite easy to see clearly underwater if you have the right tools. First, you'll need the following materials. (Ask an adult for help finding them!)

- Plastic or metal tube, at least 4" in diameter

- Clear, heavy duty plastic wrap

- 2 thick rubber bands

INSTRUCTIONS

Let's start with the tube. A clear plastic tube is best because it lets in more light, which will make it easier to see. But in a pinch, any plastic or metal tube will work. If you don't have one, you can easily make one:

1. Find an empty coffee can, or some other can of similar size. Use a can opener to trim off the bottom of the can so that you can see all the way through it. Ask an adult to crimp any sharp points down and be careful not to touch any of the remaining sharp edges inside the can.

2. Stretch a piece of heavy-duty plastic wrap tightly across the bottom of the can and use the two thick rubber bands to hold it in place. Make sure the bands are tight enough to give you a waterproof seal.

3. Once your viewing tube is finished, take it to the body of water you're interested in studying and place the end of the viewer enclosed with the wrap below the water line. Look through the top and you'll see that everything under the water is now crystal clear.

Using this tool will make your search for lost or hidden objects so much easier—and it's also a great way to spy on fish, frogs, salamanders and other denizens of the deep!

IMPORTANT NOTE
IN THE CASE OF ACTIVE WATER, MAKE SURE NOT TO VENTURE TOO FAR AWAY FROM THE SHORELINE OR INTO AREAS WHERE THE FOOTING IS BAD. THE LAST THING YOU WANT IS TO FALL INTO A FAST-MOVING BODY OF WATER!

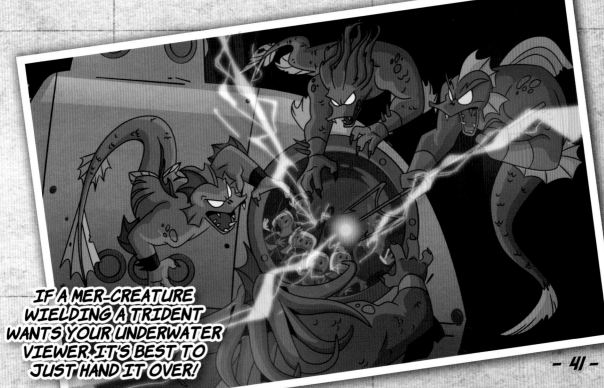

IF A MER-CREATURE WIELDING A TRIDENT WANTS YOUR UNDERWATER VIEWER, IT'S BEST TO JUST HAND IT OVER!

PAN FOR GOLD

UNCLE SCROOGE IS WELL-KNOWN FOR THE MASSIVE AMOUNTS OF GOLD HE'S COLLECTED OVER THE YEARS, MUCH OF IT FOUND DURING HIS ADVENTURES AROUND THE WORLD (AND WHEN PROSPECTING FOR HIS FORTUNE IN THE KLONDIKE DURING THE GOLD RUSH).

GOLD RUSH? WAIT, HOW OLD ARE YOU?

Finding gold of any kind takes patience and hard work. Gold coins aren't just sitting at the bottom of a stream—but tiny fragments of gold might be!

Looking for gold in a stream is called "panning." The method used by prospectors is actually pretty simple. All you're really trying to do is get the heaviest materials in the water—the gold—to settle in the bottom of the pan, while the lighter materials wash out.

FIND THAT GOLD!

FIRST, find a shallow point in a stream where the water moves quickly, but not so quickly that it's a danger to you or your friends, or that it threatens to wash out the sediment in your pan. The water should also be very clear.

HERE IS THE BASIC EQUIPMENT YOU'LL NEED

- RAIN BOOTS TO KEEP YOUR FEET DRY (NOTE: NOT REQUIRED IF YOU ARE A DUCK)

- A METAL PIE PAN (A PLASTIC OR FOIL PIE PAN CAN WORK TOO)

- AN EYE DROPPER OR TWEEZERS

- A SHALLOW BUCKET

- A QUARTER-INCH WIRE MESH SCREEN (IF YOU CAN'T FIND ANY OF THIS, IT'S OK—YOU CAN STILL PAN FOR GOLD WITHOUT IT!)

PAN FOR GOLD

FIRST, put the screen on top of your pan and scoop some of the sediment from the streambed on top of it. Shake it from side to side a bit and the smaller pieces of sediment will fall down into the pan. Put the larger pieces that remain on top of the screen into another pan or a shallow bucket and inspect the material separately, looking for larger pieces of gold. If you don't have a screen, you'll just need to pull out any pieces larger than a ¼ inch wide by hand, which can take some time. It'll be worth it when you're swimming in gold like Scrooge McDuck!

NEXT, once you've got the larger pieces separated out of the pan, lower one edge of the pan into the moving water. Don't put it in too deep, or too much of the sediment will wash away, potentially carrying away your gold fragments with it.

STRIKING IT RICH TAKES PATIENCE

NOW shake the pan from side to side at a slight angle; not too roughly—just enough to move the sediment around. Be sure not to

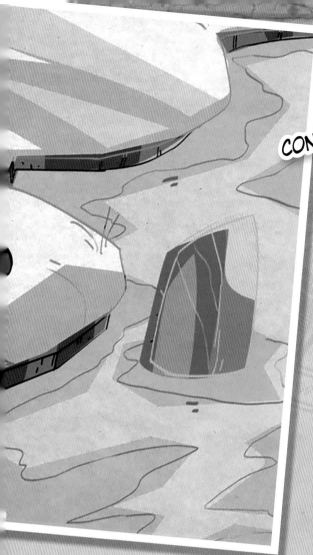

CONGRATULATIONS! YOU JUST DISCOVERED GOLD IN THEM THAR HILLS (OR STREAMS)!

wash it out of the pan just yet! The goal here is to allow heavier sediments, like gold, to settle to the bottom edge of the pan, while lighter sediments are moved to the top.

ONCE you've re-settled the sediment, lower the forward edge of the pan just below the surface of the water and start moving it around so that the water slowly washes away the topmost layers of sand. Don't try to pour out the lighter sediment yourself—let the water action do

most of the work. Once you start to see darker, heavier material at the top of the sediment, you'll have washed much of the sand and gravel away.

NOW, repeat the process. Re-settle what remains in the pan and let the water carry away the lighter material. You may need to repeat this several times, but it's the only sure way to separate out any gold. Eventually, the remaining sediment will be mostly black. Any gold in the pan will stand out due to its brighter, lighter color. Once you spot some, pick it out very carefully with an eye dropper or tweezers and put it in a plastic ziptop bag.

ADVENTURING ROCKS!

IF YOU WANT TO HAVE A LITTLE PIECE OF SOMETHING FROM EVERY ADVENTURE YOU GO ON, CONSIDER TAKING UP ROCK COLLECTING!

If you think rocks are boring, that's because you haven't looked closely enough. Each one tells you something about our planet's geological history. And plus, you never know—what looks like a rock might actually end up being a Terra-firmian!

THE ROCK CYCLE

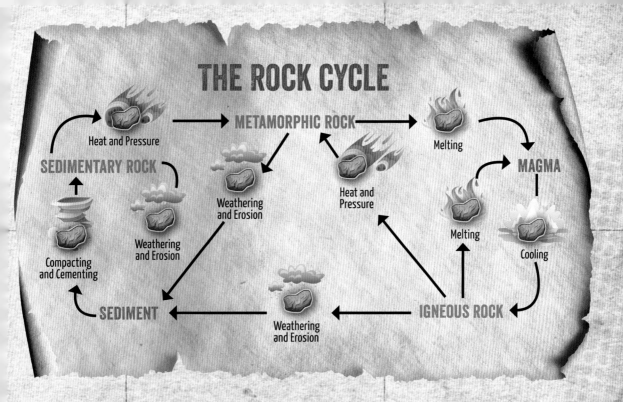

THERE ARE THREE KINDS OF ROCKS

1. IGNEOUS ROCKS

are formed when molten rock, also known as magma, cools and solidifies. If the magma cools slowly (usually that means it's happening thousands of feet below the Earth's surface), it creates a coarse-grained rock. If it's at the Earth's surface and cools quickly—probably after a volcano eruption—it creates a fine-grained rock.

2. METAMORPHIC ROCKS

are formed when igneous or sedimentary rocks are exposed to extremely high temperatures or pressures, or very large amounts of hot water. This "metamorphosis" makes the rocks denser and more compact.

3. SEDIMENTARY ROCKS

are constantly being formed all around us. They are created by layers of sediment and other rock fragments, minerals and even plant and animal material. The layers of most sedimentary rocks become joined together by minerals and chemicals.

WITH ENOUGH TIME, ANY ONE OF THESE KINDS OF ROCKS CAN TRANSFORM INTO ONE OF THE OTHERS!

ADVENTURING ROCKS!

SILTSTONE

SANDSTONE

Because sedimentary rocks are the ones most commonly formed on the surface of the Earth, they're the ones you're most likely to find. (Though as Huey knows, tremors can expose all different kinds of rocks.) See if you can find any of these sedimentary rocks while you're out adventuring—but definitely not while exploring abandoned subway tunnels because that would not be safe!

CONGLOMERATE

FOSSILIFEROUS LIMESTONE

ROCK SALT

COAL

LIMESTONE

ARKOSE

MUDSTONE

SHALE

TRAVERTINE

ROCK GYPSUM

FOSSIL FACTS

YOU CAN'T ACTUALLY TRAVEL TO PREHISTORIC TIMES, BUT EXAMINING FOSSILS WILL GIVE YOU A GOOD IDEA OF WHAT THEY WERE LIKE!

WHAT ARE FOSSILS?

Fossils are remains of animals or plants from at least 10,000 years ago. Most organisms don't become fossils after they die—the conditions have to be just right. If left exposed, the remains will decay. But if they happen to sink into mud, the lack of air will keep that from happening. If the remains are undisturbed for thousands (or even millions!) of years, more mud will press down on them. Eventually, minerals dissolved in the mud will harden the remains, turning them to stone.

Fossils can also form in a couple other ways. Paleontologists, who are scientists looking for fossils, have discovered insects, small animals, plants and even dinosaur feathers from millions of years ago trapped inside amber, which is fossilized tree resin.

The other common type of fossil is an imprint. Plants, animal tracks and footprints are most often fossilized this way. If an animal walks over clay before it has dried, it will leave an impression that can last for millions of years. Similarly, if a plant is covered by sediment, the plant will eventually degrade, but an imprint will be left where the leaf was.

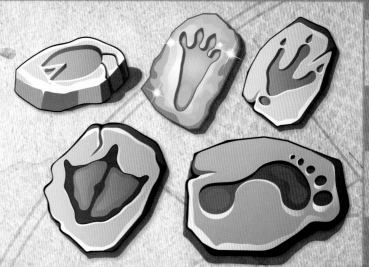

And though they're not technically fossils, animals or people who get trapped in ice can be naturally "mummified." It takes a lot longer than the five years Scrooge and Goldie were trapped in ice in the Golden Lagoon of White Agony Plains, though—"ice mummies" can be as old as the Ice Age!

FOSSIL FACTS

WHY ARE FOSSILS COOL?

Fossils are awesome because they can help us understand what life was like on Earth thousands and thousands of years ago. Most famously, fossils give us hints about what dinosaurs were like!

FINDING FOSSILS

Searching for fossils can make for an excellent adventure! Fossils are especially common in Colorado, Utah, Wyoming and Montana, but that doesn't mean you can't find one in your backyard—fossils have been found all over the United States (and the rest of the world, too).

  If you don't live near any famous fossil sites, you can probably check out fossils at a natural history museum or fancy gala. Hopefully no thieving ex-girlfriends of Scrooge's have stolen the skulls!

LA BREA TAR PITS

In the middle of Los Angeles is a sort of natural time capsule. Natural asphalt bubbles up, creating "tar pits" that have trapped animals for tens of thousands of years! More than 3.5 million fossils have been discovered there—scientists continue to excavate them year round. You can visit the tar pits and see everything from mollusks to mountain lions to mammoths! But you probably won't see any dinosaurs. The oldest fossils found there are from 50,000 years ago—a full 65 million years after the Age of Dinosaurs ended.

D.C. DINOS

An amatuer paleontologist named Ray Stanford made an amazing discovery in local stream beds near Washington, D.C., where he found almost 900 Middle Cretaceous dinosaur tracks in the area's rocks! Professional paleontologists were amazed— they didn't think dinosaur tracks existed in that area. Ray donated his findings to the National Museum of Natural History in Washington, D.C., so all adventurers could enjoy them.

DUCK-BILLED DINOSAURS

The oldest-known duck-billed dinosaur, called a hadrosaur, was found in Texas. The 95.5 million-year-old fossils from a *Protohadros byrdi* have made some scientists question whether hadrosaurs were actually native to North America—previously, scientists believed Asia was their birthplace.

RESPECT YOUR ELDER!

CURIOUS CRITTERS

ALWAYS BE ON THE LOOKOUT FOR SNAKES AND INSECTS, EVEN ONES THAT ONLY EXIST IN YOUR DREAMS! AND IF ONE DOES SHOW UP IN YOUR DREAM, MAKE SURE YOU DEFEAT IT, OR IT COULD BREAK OUT OF THE DREAM!

SURPRISING SNAKES

Snakes slither on every continent except Antartica, so you're bound to see one sooner or later!

NO EYELIDS

Unlike humans (and ducks!), a snake never closes its eyes. The eyes of a snake are instead protected by a clear membrane called a brille, which removes the need for blinking.

FLEXIBLE JAWS

Snakes have the ability to swallow prey that is much larger than themselves. This is thanks to their unusual jaws. The snake's lower jaw is divided into two independently moving halves that allow it to stretch to an incredible size!

FROM MEGA TO MINI

The world's largest snake is the green anaconda, which can grow to be 29 feet long and weigh 550 pounds. In contrast, the Barbados threadsnake is the world's smallest, at only 10 centimeters long.

INTERESTING INSECTS

All insects are fascinating creatures—even ones that aren't as rare as the Duckburg Giant Butterfly!

IS IT AN INSECT OR AN ARACHNID?

Insects possess a head, a middle called an abdomen and an end referred to as a thorax. Due to their lack of an abdomen, spiders are not insects—they're part of a classification called arachnids. Scorpions are arachnids too!

THEY'VE BEEN AROUND FOR A LONG TIME!

The most ancient insect fossil is more than 400 million years old. Not only does this mean that insects are older than dinosaurs, it also means they might have been some of the first land-based creatures.

HIVE SOCIETIES

Many species of insects, such as bees and ants, live in very complicated societies. Every member of the hive has a specific role, usually in service to a queen. Most of the hive's working populace is female, and many engage in a form of farming. Some ant hives have been known to go to war with each other! Also, bees don't like it when you steal their hives.

THEY'RE THE WORLD'S MOST POPULOUS CRITTERS

Of the 1.5 million species discovered by scientists, two-thirds have been insects.

HIGH SEAS ADVENTURES

DIVE INTO ADVENTURES AT SEA!
YOU DON'T NEED TO GO ALL
THE WAY TO ATLANTIS TO SEE SOME
INCREDIBLE SIGHTS. FIND OUT
HOW TO USE MORSE CODE, TALK
LIKE A SAILOR, MANEUVER A
CANOE AND MORE!

PREPARE FOR A DAY AT SEA

BEFORE PACKING FOR YOUR TRIP ON THE WATER, MAKE SURE YOU KNOW WHERE YOU'RE HEADED AND WHAT YOU'RE LIKELY TO FIND THERE.

Are there any legends or stories associated with the area? Perhaps lost ships or giant sea serpents? What about ghost pirates, like Captain Peghook, or buried treasure? Knowing the history of the area you'll be exploring will help you get the most out of your trip.

Savvy adventurers prepare for anything and everything, but here's a list of the basics that you should take along....

THINGS TO INCLUDE

- FRESH DRINKING WATER
(YES, WATER IS ALL AROUND YOU,
BUT IF YOU'RE ON THE OCEAN,
YOU WON'T BE ABLE TO DRINK IT)

- A LIFE JACKET
(THIS IS A MUST)

- SUNSCREEN

- SWIMSUIT

- FISHING POLE AND BAIT

- A GOOD BOOK TO READ

- HOT DOG COSTUME

*IN CASE WE GET LOST AT SEA
AND ONE OF US, PROBABLY
LOUIE, GOES MAD WITH HUNGER,
WE'LL PUT THESE ON.*

PREPARE FOR A DAY AT SEA

IF YOU WANT TO DO MORE THAN LIE ON A DECK OR PADDLE AROUND, YOU'LL NEED SOME EXTRA GEAR.

There are plenty of exciting adventures to be had at sea—it pays to be prepared for all of them!

- An **UNDERWATER VIEWER**, perfect for spotting creatures and treasures in shallow waters (see pg. 38 for construction details).

- A **CAMERA** for taking pictures of unexpected sea life or unexpected money sharks.

- **BINOCULARS**—just what you need to spot pirate ships (or planes) before they get too close.

- A **CB RADIO** in case you need to signal for help (see pg. 63 to learn Morse code).

- A **LIST OF NAUTICAL TERMINOLOGY,** which will enable you to speak the lingo of others at sea (see pg. 64). There's more to it than "arrrrr matey!"

AHOY, SKY PIRATES
KEEP AN EYE TO THE SKIES WHILE YOU'RE AT SEA, JUST IN CASE ANY SKY PIRATES ARE HOVERING AROUND! BUT DON'T GET DISTRACTED BY THEIR TERRIFIC SONG AND DANCE ROUTINES, OR THEY'LL ROB YOUR VESSEL OF EVERYTHING IT'S CARRYING!

MORSE CODE!

MORSE CODE IS A SIMPLE SUBSTITUTION ALPHABET THAT CONSISTS OF "DOTS" AND "DASHES." IT'S ESPECIALLY HANDY TO KNOW IF YOU'RE ON A PLANE OR HELICOPTER THAT LAUNCHPAD IS PILOTING, AS YOU NEVER KNOW WHEN ONE OF HIS "LANDINGS" WILL REQUIRE YOU TO SIGNAL FOR A RESCUE MISSION.

Dots are short bursts of either light or sound, while dashes are longer. When written down, dots and dashes appear as just that—a series of dots and dashes. So if you want to communicate at night, you can spell out words using long and short bursts from a flashlight directed toward the person with whom you want to communicate. Make sure to pause between each word, so that the recipient knows where each one begins and ends.

The table to the right details International Morse Code, including letters, numbers and punctuation. Be sure to share it with anyone you want to talk to in code.

A	B	C	D	E	F
·−	−···	−·−·	−··	·	··−·
G	H	I	J	K	L
−−·	····	··	·−−−	−·−	·−··
M	N	O	P	Q	R
−−	−·	−−−	·−−·	−−·−	·−·
S	T	U	V	W	X
···	−	··−	···−	·−−	−··−
Y	Z	0	1	2	3
−·−−	−−··	−−−−−	·−−−−	··−−−	···−−
4	5	6	7	8	9
····−	·····	−····	−−···	−−−··	−−−−·
.	)	?	`	!	/
·−·−·−	−·−−·−	··−−··	·−−−−·	−·−·−−	−··−·
(	)	&	:	;	=
−·−−·	−·−−·−	·−···	−−−···	−·−·−·	−···−
+	−	_	"	$	@
·−·−·	−····−	··−−·−	·−··−·	···−··−	·−−·−·

··· −−− ··· = SOS

MORSE CODE GUIDE

1 DASH = 3 DOTS

THE SPACE BETWEEN PARTS OF THE SAME LETTER = 1 DOT

THE SPACE BETWEEN LETTERS = 3 DOTS

THE SPACE BETWEEN WORDS = 7 DOTS

TALK LIKE A SEA CAPTAIN

IF YOU'RE GOING TO SAIL AROUND THE WORLD LOOKING FOR ADVENTURE, YOU'LL NEED TO KNOW HOW TO TALK WHILE YOU'RE ON A BOAT—ESPECIALLY IF YOU ENCOUNTER PIRATES. (EVEN ONES WHO SAIL THE SKIES AND NOT THE SEA.)

ABOARD To be on a ship.

AHOY Said to grab attention, as in, "Ahoy, matey!"

ANCHOR A heavy metal object thrown overboard to keep the ship in place.

BATTEN DOWN THE HATCHES Prepare the ship for a storm.

BOW The front of the ship.

HARDTACK A kind of hard biscuit meant to last for long journeys.

HULL The framework of the ship.

JACK A sailor or a flag.

KNOT A unit of speed, one nautical mile per hour (about 1.15 miles).

LANDLUBBER A person who is not comfortable aboard a ship.

PIRATE A sea robber or criminal.

PORT When facing the bow,
the left side of the ship.

SHIVER ME TIMBERS
An expression that means you're very surprised.

STARBOARD When facing the bow,
the right side of the ship.

STERN The back of the ship.

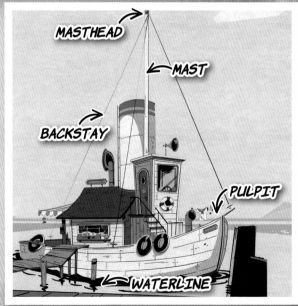

MASTHEAD
MAST
BACKSTAY
PULPIT
WATERLINE

MANEUVER A CANOE

FIRST THINGS FIRST

Anytime you get into a canoe, make sure you're wearing a life jacket of appropriate size. It should fit snugly. Also, make sure your parents have given you permission to go canoeing, that the water isn't too cold and that there's an adult nearby in case of an emergency. Finally, don't move your canoe into any fast-moving water without an experienced adult on board who can steer you out of it or get you through it safely.

And one last thing—don't get lost, or your adventure buddies will call you Captain Lost for the rest of time!

GETTING STARTED

Always canoe with an adventure buddy (or two). One of you will be the bowman. This person sits in the front of the canoe and keeps an eye out for any obstacles. The other person will be the sternman, who sits in the back of the canoe and does most of the steering. The sternman also lets the bowman know what side of the canoe to paddle on and when. Both are important jobs! A third can paddle along with the bowman, or they can not paddle at all.

Before getting into the canoe, make sure it's secured to the dock. If you're at a shoreline rather than a dock, just make sure a buddy is holding the canoe steady as you get in. The bowman sits in the front of the canoe, while the sternman sits in the back.

GET MOVING

Grab the top end of the paddle with your "inside" hand. This is the hand that will be farthest from the water as you paddle. Your other hand will grab the paddle about two feet from the top. If you switch your paddle to the other side of the boat, you'll need to remember to switch your hand position as well.

Put the blade of the paddle in the water ahead of where you're sitting and pull it back with your lower hand in a smooth motion. The blade should stay underwater and be angled outward in order to push against the water as you paddle. Once you can't pull the paddle back any more, move it over the water to the front position again and repeat the motion.

Once both of you are seated, untie your canoe from the dock and push off with your hand. If you're on the shore, rather than a dock, wait until the bowman is seated and then the sternman, who gets into the canoe last, will have to push off with his or her foot as he or she's getting into the canoe. This takes good balance, so be careful and don't rush!

At the same time, your fellow adventurer will need to paddle on the opposite side of the canoe. Time your strokes together for maximum efficiency and power. It's up to the sternman to adjust his strokes to match the pace of the bowman. And remember, there's no need to go super-fast! Keep it slow and steady, and try to avoid hitting any rocks!

MANEUVER A CANOE

TURNING YOUR CANOE

To turn the canoe, the sternman needs to make a small backward stroke in the shape of a "J." To do this, put your paddle in the water as you would with any stroke, then, once you've pulled the paddle all the way back, sweep it outward and away from the boat in a J-like hook. If you do this on the left side of the boat, you'll go left. On the right side, you'll head right.

   If you need to make a sharper turn to the right or left, it's easiest for the sternman to do it. You should hold your paddle out to the side of the canoe, straight up and down, with the flat face of the blade in the water and parallel to the boat. Pull the blade toward the boat and the boat will turn. If you execute this move on the left-hand side of the boat, you'll turn right. If you do it on the right side of the boat, you'll turn left.

LANDING YOUR CANOE

Landing your canoe on the shoreline is easy—just paddle directly into the shore. The bowman gets out first, then holds the craft steady for the sternman to get out. If you're landing at a dock, paddle close enough so that your canoe is parallel with the dock itself. Then steady the craft and get out carefully, one at a time. Hold the canoe for one another to ensure it doesn't drift away from the dock as you're trying to exit. And don't forget to tie it up or put it away!

WHAT TO DO IF YOUR CANOE FLIPS

If your canoe flips over with you in it, your best option is to grab ahold of the canoe and try swimming to shore with it. If you can save your paddles by shoving them under the seats, that's great news, but if you can't reach them, get to shore and right the canoe while you're standing on dry land. The safety of you and your adventure buddy is the most important thing, so if you need to let go of the canoe and the paddles in order to get back to shore safely, then do it.

If your canoe tips in a spot where the current is strong, hold onto the canoe until the water slows down, and then make for shore.

If you're far from the shore and with a friend, you can try flipping the canoe upright. You take one end of the canoe and have your friend take the other. Lift it up as high out of the water as possible and then both of you should try and flip it in the same direction. With some luck, it will land on its side and roll upright. Getting back in presents its own challenges because you won't be able to climb in from the side without tipping the canoe back over again. Instead, try pulling yourself up and over the front and back ends of the canoe, one at a time, working to hold the canoe steady during each person's attempt at getting in.

ONWARD! TO ADVENTURE!

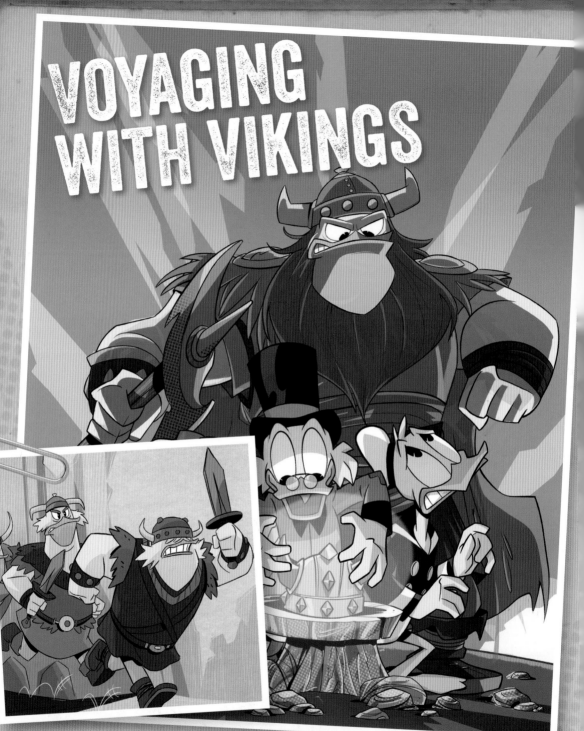

VOYAGING WITH VIKINGS

DONALD AND SCROOGE MET VIKINGS ON ONE OF THEIR ADVENTURES—AND THEY WERE LUCKY TO GET AWAY UNHARMED!

EXCELLENT EXPLORERS

Vikings were fierce explorers from Scandinavia (now known as Norway, Sweden and Denmark). The Viking Age, when they were most active and raided and plundered other countries, lasted from about 700 to 1100 A.D. Vikings were expert shipbuilders and sailors—in fact, they were the first Europeans to reach America, about 500 years before Christopher Columbus!

SUPERB SAILORS

Vikings built longships, or light, slender ships that moved very quickly in the water. They often carved snakes or dragons onto the fronts of their ships to scare anyone who saw them coming (and to keep onlookers from confusing them with cruise ships). Most longships were 50–120 feet long and had between 24 and 50 oars. Keels along the bottoms of the boats made them easy to steer, and they were made to float high on the water, which made it easy for the vikings to land on beaches.

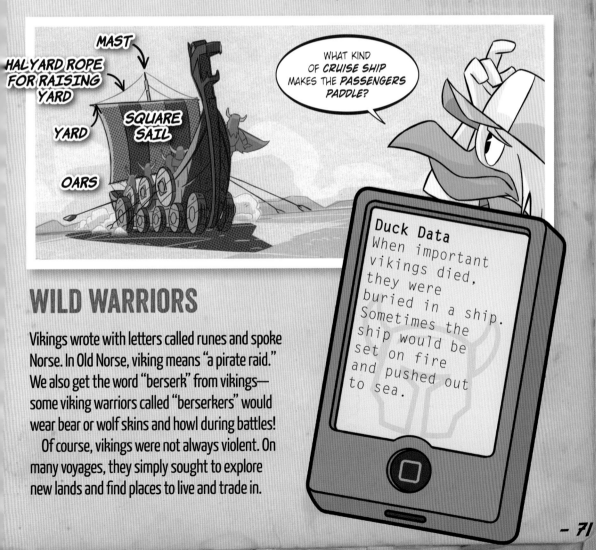

WILD WARRIORS

Vikings wrote with letters called runes and spoke Norse. In Old Norse, viking means "a pirate raid." We also get the word "berserk" from vikings— some viking warriors called "berserkers" would wear bear or wolf skins and howl during battles!

Of course, vikings were not always violent. On many voyages, they simply sought to explore new lands and find places to live and trade in.

MYSTERIOUS ADVENTURES

YOU NEED TO BE PREPARED IN CASE SOME OF YOUR ADVENTURES WIND UP BEING OTHERWORLDLY! DISCOVER HOW TO LOOK FOR GHOSTS, DETECT SECRET DOORS AND COMPARTMENTS, EXPLORE IN THE DARK AND MUCH MORE! (IT'LL BE USEFUL IF YOU ACCIDENTALLY RELEASE A GHOST IN YOUR UNCLE'S WING OF SECRETS).

SOLVING A MYSTERY

SOLVING A MYSTERY IS ALL ABOUT LOOKING AT THE BIG PICTURE. ONE OF THE EASIEST WAYS TO DO THAT IS TO MAKE AN INVESTIGATION BOARD, LIKE THE ONE WEBBY MADE WITH ALL THE INFORMATION SHE COULD FIND ON SCROOGE McDUCK. YOU CAN MAKE ONE TOO!

Using a bulletin board and push pins, put up all the evidence you have, such as photographs and newspaper articles. You can also include questions and theories written out on pieces of paper. Use colored string to show connections between different pieces of evidence— you might even see a connection that you didn't notice before.

GREAT, MYSTERY SOLVED— NOW WHAT?

DETECT SECRET DOORS AND COMPARTMENTS

HEROES AND VILLAINS ALIKE USE HIDDEN DOORS AND STORAGE SPACES FOR LOTS OF REASONS—TO STORE TREASURE, HIDE EVIDENCE OF THEIR WRONGDOING OR JUST OBSCURE THE ENTRANCE TO A HIDDEN, PRIVATE CHAMBER. UNCLE SCROOGE USES ONE OF HIS TO HIDE HIS PRIVATE OFFICE. SECRET DOORS, SHELVES AND SAFES CAN BE PRETTY DIFFICULT TO FIND. THAT'S WHAT MAKES THEM A SECRET!

1. NOTICE IRREGULARITIES

Some places are more likely than others to hide a false bottom or secret door. If you notice something's out of order, like Dewey and Webby did in Scrooge's library, try fixing it. It could lead to a secret room!

2. FIND A KEY

Other secret areas, like Scrooge's other bin, might require you to find something special to get in. If you're in a Wing of Secrets, check objects for hidden levers and knobs that could release a hidden key, like the one Webby found in this pole.

DETECT SECRET DOORS AND COMPARTMENTS

3. POKE AROUND

You can also try to find the secret door by pulling on books (like Dewey accidentally did when being chased by a demon), pushing gently on panel seams and looking behind mirrors and paintings. Keep in mind that a plainly painted wall without any patterns or seams is probably just a wall. But a wall with a few lumps in it? That's worth looking into.

EXTRA TIP!
IF YOU FEEL A BREEZE, THERE MIGHT BE A HIDDEN PASSAGE!

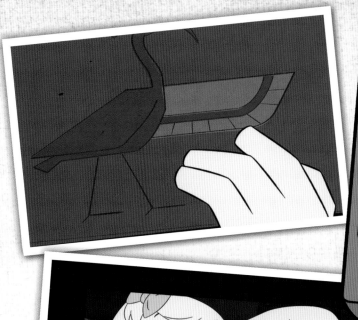

WHEN WEBBY AND LOUIE WERE LOST IN THE PYRAMID OF TOTH-RA, THEY FOUND A SECRET PASSAGE BY PRESSING ON A HIEROGLYPH!

ENHANCING YOUR SENSES

WHEN YOU'RE ON A MYSTERIOUS ADVENTURE WHERE YOU CAN HARDLY BELIEVE WHAT YOU'RE SEEING, YOU NEED TO KNOW YOU CAN TRUST YOUR SENSES!

Here are a few tips to make sure you're at the top of your game, whether you're listening for the sounds of a sky pirate about to launch into song or you think you just saw your friends leap through a wormhole at the top of Mt. Neverrest.

SUPERIOR SIGHT

1. *EAT UP.* Foods high in vitamins A, C and E are good for improving your vision. Dark leafy greens, pumpkin and carrots are all good choices.

2. *STAY AWAY FROM SCREENS.* Staring at your phone or computer all day is a real strain on your eyes—we're guessing Mark Beaks is going blind! If you're working on a project, make sure to take a break at least once an hour.

3. *EXERCISE THOSE EYES.* A simple eye roll can help you focus your vision. Look up, to the side, down and then to the other side. Repeat 10 times.

SELECTIVE SNIFFER

1. INHALE STRONG SMELLS.
Spend a few minutes each day sniffing things like perfume, flowers or fresh cut grass. After a few weeks, your nose will be able to pick up on them more easily.

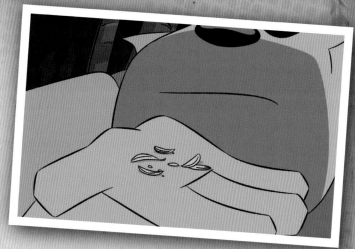

2. QUIZ YOUR NOSE. Close your eyes and have a friend hold different scented candles or foods under your nose. Take turns seeing who can get the most right!

3. ZINC UP! Foods like beef, spinach and pumpkin seeds are all high in zinc, which is good for your sense of smell.

HIGH LEVEL HEARING

1. LISTEN TO MUSIC. Try listening to jazz with headphones at a medium to low volume, and see if you can pick out all the different instruments. DJ helmets are not recommended.

2. STAY AWAY FROM LOUD NOISES. Super loud concerts can leave you with a ringing in your ears— that's not helpful on any adventure! If you will be around loud noises, bring ear plugs.

3. AN APPLE A DAY KEEPS THE EAR DOCTOR AWAY! Apples are full of an antioxidant called quercetin, which can help protect your hearing.

EXPLORE IN THE DARK

WEBBY'S ALWAYS PREPARED IN THE DARK—SHE EVEN HAS A DART GUN! MAKE SURE YOU'RE PREPARED, TOO.

FLASHLIGHT

Be sure to pack replacement batteries and bulbs.

Make sure you're proficient at changing bulbs and batteries in total darkness. This will be a necessary skill if your flashlight dies when you can't see anything.

In a pinch, you can use the flashlight on your phone, like Lena did in the abandoned subway.

MAP OF THE AREA, IF ONE EXISTS

Familiarize yourself with the map prior to your adventure. That way you'll have some sense of where you are, even if you aren't able to look at it on a regular basis.

BALL OF STRING OR A LONG REEL OF FISHING LINE

You'll run this line along the wall or along the ground when you move into chambers that might have multiple exits or a confusing layout, like the Temple of Heroes in Ithaquack. Otherwise, you might need to ask a giant sea monster for directions.

CHALK

If you run out of line, or are venturing farther than a line will allow, you can use chalk to mark directions when faced with options for which way to go. The chalk will enable you to draw an arrow or other symbol on the wall, indicating the right way back home.

1. CONSERVE YOUR FLASHLIGHT BATTERY AS MUCH AS POSSIBLE. If each of you and your friends brought a flashlight, don't use them all at the same time!

2. BE ALERT! Make sure to check your footing and what's in front of you, particularly at head height. You'll want to make sure you don't step into any holes, trip over anything on the ground or hit your head on any low-hanging branches or overhangs.

3. LET AN ADULT KNOW ANYTIME YOU GO EXPLORING IN THE DARK. And let them know what time you'll be back. Whispering it as you walk away doesn't count!

CHECK FOR TRAPS

IF YOU'RE WANDERING AROUND ATLANTIS OR THE TEMPLE OF MONTEPLUMAGE, THERE'S A POSSIBILITY IT'S BEEN OUTFITTED WITH EXTRA FEATURES DESIGNED TO KEEP PEOPLE OUT. AS WEBBY SAYS, "RULE NUMBER 1: IF YOU THINK IT MIGHT BE CURSED, DON'T TOUCH IT!" IF YOU REALLY THINK A ROOM MIGHT BE BOOBY TRAPPED, GET OUT OF THERE! AND EVEN IF YOU THINK IT'S SAFE, TREAD WITH CAUTION.

1. LOOK AROUND VERY CAREFULLY

See if you can spot any laser tripwires, blinking lights or anything else that looks suspicious.

EXTRA TIP
TOSS A BALL OR ROCK INTO THE AREA! IF THE TRAPS ARE ACTIVATED BY MOTION, THEN THIS MIGHT SET THEM OFF.

2. AGAIN: DON'T TOUCH ANYTHING YOU DON'T HAVE TO

As Dewey found out when he went to Atlantis, many booby traps are set off by things such as turning on lights or picking up objects—like the decoy Jewel of Atlantis. Bring your own flashlight, and resist the urge to poke around places where you don't have to!

3. STEP LIGHTLY

Slowly test your weight with every step. If you're walking on a rug or carpet, it could be hiding a giant hole! And even wood and stone floors can have trap doors.

LET'S HUNT FOR A GHOST!

YOU MIGHT SUSPECT THAT THERE'S A GHOST IN THE AREA, BUT PROVING IT EXISTS COULD BE TRICKY. (UNLESS, LIKE WEBBY, YOU ACCIDENTALLY UNLEASH ONE IN SCROOGE'S WING OF SECRETS!)

First, be sure to approach the challenge as if you were a scientist. Use critical thinking and a logical scientific method to prove or disprove everything. Make no assumptions! Eliminate all possible natural causes of what appears to be a haunting before making any assumptions about supernatural involvement.

JUST BECAUSE IT'S A MYTH DOESN'T MEAN IT'S NOT TRUE!

HERE'S SOME EQUIPMENT YOU'LL NEED AND TIPS FOR HOW TO USE IT

- **A DIGITAL RECORDER**
  Most smartphones have one built in—if you don't have one, ask your parents if you can use theirs, or see if you can find one that isn't part of a phone. Use the recorder to try and catch creepy sounds or whispers that occur without explanation.

- **A DIGITAL CAMERA**
  Most smartphones also include a camera, but you can use any camera you have access to. Use the camera to take pictures in the light to look for any evidence of spirit forms that can't be seen with the naked eye. You can also take photos in the dark to try and capture unexplained lights.

- **A NOTEPAD AND PEN**
  You'll want to make a note about anything unusual so that you'll have a record of evidence related to the haunting. You'll also want to write down when no evidence could be found.

- **SERIOUS SNACKS AND WATER**
  Ghost-hunting is thirsty, hungry work. Be sure you're prepared to keep your energy up since some of your investigation might be taking place at night.

Once you've collected your evidence, review your notes. Could any of the effects you confirmed be caused by other means? Think hard—and challenge any assumptions you might be making. If all evidence points toward the unexplainable, it may be that you've discovered an actual ghost!

SNEAK, DON'T SPEAK

MOVING QUIETLY CAN COME IN HANDY IN LOTS OF SITUATIONS—LIKE WHEN YOU'RE SNEAKING AWAY FROM YOUR UNCLE, TRYING TO STEALTHILY RETREAT FROM THE BEAGLE BOYS, OR EVEN WHEN YOU'RE PLAYING HIDE AND SEEK! FOLLOW THESE TIPS, AND YOU'LL BE THE SNEAKIEST ADVENTURER AROUND.

1. WEAR SOFT CLOTHING

Don't wear pants made of "swishy" material, or a zip up sweatshirt—nothing's louder than the sound of that metal zipper clanking on a doorknob!

2. WALK CLOSE TO WALLS

Not only will this make it a little harder to see you if someone glances in the room, wooden floors are usually better supported near the walls, so it's less likely that you'll step on a creaky spot. This is true when walking up stairs as well. Stay next to the walls to move as silently as possible.

SUCH GOOD BOYS.

3. WEAR SOFT-SOLED SHOES AND WALK LIGHTLY

They don't call them "sneakers" for nothing! You're sure to be heard if you go clunking around in heavy-bottomed shoes, so stick to trainers or rubber-soled shoes. Avoid flip-flops at all costs! They're named after the sound they make.

OR SKIP SHOES IF YOU'RE INDOORS!

4. WALK ON BARE DIRT AND FRESH GRASS

If you're outside, try to avoid walking on gravel or through fallen leaves, which will definitely crunch when you step on them.

5. WALK HEEL TO TOE

Be mindful of every step, always placing your heel down quietly and slowly rolling your foot to your toes.

Duck Data
If you want to be super stealthy, think like a ninja! Real ninjas didn't wear all black and cover their faces. Lots of ninja strongholds were in rural areas, so they often dressed as farmers—looking like you belong is the best way to blend in!

ADVENTURING AROUND THE WORLD

TRUE ADVENTURERS KNOW THERE ARE WONDERS TO BE SEEN ALL OVER THE WORLD! DISCOVER HOW TO INTRODUCE YOURSELF TO NEW PEOPLE, DRESS FOR ANY ENVIRONMENT AND LEARN ABOUT CULTURES AROUND THE GLOBE, FROM SCOTLAND TO THE PYRAMIDS AND BEYOND!

BELIEVE IT OR NOT, SOCIAL SKILLS COME IN VERY HANDY FOR ADVENTURERS! YOU'RE BOUND TO NEED HELP FROM TIME TO TIME WHEN YOU'RE EXPLORING NEW PLACES, AND PEOPLE (EVEN MUMMIES!) WILL BE MUCH MORE LIKELY TO HELP YOU IF THEY LIKE YOU.

1. SMILE!

Approaching someone with a smile on your face tells them that you're friendly—not threatening.

2. ASK A QUESTION

Ask something that isn't too personal. "Where are you from?" and "What brings you here?" are good openers. After you've done that, you can ask questions such as "Do you know the way to the hidden chamber?" or "Do you know any fun places to explore around here?"

ENCOUNTERING NEW PEOPLE

3. OFFER THEM FOODS THEY'VE NEVER TRIED BEFORE

Exchanging food is a sign of good will, and it's proven to get results. When Uncle Scrooge needed help rescuing Webby and Louie from the Lost Pyramid of Toth-Ra's hidden chamber, they couldn't convince the mummies to help them until Launchpad let them try his burrito!

I'M NOT TRYING TO BE AMAZING, IT JUST COMES NATURALLY.

DUCK IN A STRANGE LAND

IF YOU'RE IN A DIFFERENT COUNTRY, YOU CAN STILL FOLLOW THESE RULES ABOUT BEING CHARMING, BUT YOU SHOULD PAY EXTRA ATTENTION TO HOW EVERYONE ELSE IS ACTING AND FOLLOW SUIT. DIFFERENT CULTURES HAVE DIFFERENT IDEAS ABOUT WHAT'S RUDE. FOR EXAMPLE, IN THE UNITED STATES (AND A LOT OF OTHER PLACES), YOU MIGHT GIVE SOMEONE A THUMBS UP TO MEAN "GOT IT!" BUT IN PARTS OF WEST AFRICA, IRAN AND GREECE, GIVING A THUMBS UP IS VERY OFFENSIVE. SO MAKE SURE TO RESEARCH LOCAL MANNERS AND GESTURES BEFORE YOU TRAVEL SOMEWHERE NEW!

DRESS FOR ANY ENVIRONMENT

WHETHER YOU'RE RUNNING FROM THE MUMMIES OF TOTH-RA IN EGYPT OR VENTURING TO THE UNDERWATER CITY OF ATLANTIS, YOU NEED TO MAKE SURE YOU HAVE THE RIGHT GEAR!

YOU'LL NEED

- A HAT
- SUNGLASSES
- A FLEECE PULLOVER
- A T-SHIRT
- LONG, LOOSE PANTS

THE DESERT

When you're in the desert put your sunglasses on right away, or like Amunet, you'll think the sun god is angry at you! Keep the pullover in your backpack for the evening. Deserts are hot during the day but can get very cold at night. And long pants will protect your legs from the elements, such as the sun and prickly plants.

UNDERWATER

Undersea adventures are tons of fun, but they need lots of special equipment! Definitely go with an expert who can make sure you're properly prepared—and if you're lucky, one who can teach you underwater golf!

YOU'LL NEED

- A WETSUIT
- GOGGLES
- A SCUBA TANK
- FLIPPERS

THE ARCTIC

If you're going to be the first adventurer to reach the top of Mt. Neverrest, the best thing you can do is stay dry and warm! Choose waterproof boots and pants, if you can—snow does melt!

YOU'LL NEED:

- A HEAVY COAT
- A WARM TOP
- A T-SHIRT
- BOOTS
- SUN GOGGLES (SEE PG. 36)
- A HAT, SCARF AND GLOVES

FOREIGN LANGUAGE BASICS

WHETHER YOU'VE BEEN VISITING ITHAQUACK OR YOU'RE JUST HAVING A HARD TIME UNDERSTANDING YOUR SCOTTISH UNCLE, IT'S ALWAYS USEFUL TO LEARN A FEW PHRASES IN ANOTHER LANGUAGE!

GABBING IN GREEK

Καλημέρα (ka-li-ME-ra): *GOOD MORNING*

Ευχαριστώ (eff-kha-ri-STOE): *THANK YOU*

Συγνώμη (See-GHNO-mee): *SORRY*

Γειά σου (YAH-soo): *HELLO*

Ναί (neh): *YES*

όχι (OH-hee): *NO*

Μιλάτε αγγλικά (mi-LA-te a-gli-KA): *DO YOU SPEAK ENGLISH?*

Δεν καταλαβαίνω (then ka-ta-la-VE-noh): *I DON'T UNDERSTAND*

A LITTLE BIT OF EGYPTIAN ARABIC

Hi, ezayik: *HI, HOW ARE YOU?*

Ma'a el Salama: *GOODBYE*

Sabah el-kheir: *GOOD MORNING*

Aiwa: *YES*

La: *NO*

Shukran: *THANK YOU*

Assif: *SORRY*

'Afuann: *YOU'RE WELCOME*

SPEAKING IN SCOTS

Whit like? (what like): *HOW ARE YOU?*

Whaur ye fae (whaddya fay): *WHERE ARE YOU FROM?*

Guid mornin (Good mornin'): *GOOD MORNING*

A dinna unnerstaun (ah dunnay unnerstawn): *I DON'T UNDERSTAND*

Dae ye talk English? (do-yeh talk English): *DO YOU SPEAK ENGLISH?*

Ay, a wee bit (eye, a wee but): *A LITTLE BIT*

Ay (eye): *YES*

Naw (noh): *NO*

ANCIENT EGYPT FACTS

IF YOU EVER FIND YOURSELF TRAPPED IN A PYRAMID FULL OF LIVING MUMMIES, IT'LL PAY TO BE FAMILIAR WITH THEIR CULTURE!

The civilization of Ancient Egypt lasted for about 3,000 years, from 3100 B.C. to 30 B.C.

Some Ancient Egyptian scribes wrote using hieroglyphics. Archaeologists couldn't translate their writings until they found the Rosetta Stone in 1799 A.D., which had the same text written in hieroglyphics, another Ancient Egyptian script known as Demotic script, and in Ancient Greek. Because scholars knew Ancient Greek, they were able to decipher the hieroglyphics—but it took them 20 years!

If someone was important and rich, they could pay to be mummified upon their death. Mummification was a long and special process of preserving someone's body—Ancient Egyptians believed after death, a person's soul left their body and journeyed to other worlds, but that the soul would have to return to the body to "recharge." Preserving the body was necessary so the soul could recognize it.

Everyone, men included, wore makeup in Ancient Egypt. People believed it had healing powers, and it also helped protect their faces from the sun.

Duck Data

If you unfurled all the bandages from a mummy, they would be about a mile long!

PHENOMENAL PYRAMIDS

Ancient Egyptians are perhaps best known for their pyramids. Built as tombs for pharaohs (Ancient Egyptian leaders) and their families, there are about 130 pyramids in Egypt! Burial chambers were filled with treasure and other items the pharaoh would be able to use in the afterlife. To trick robbers, pyramids often had lots of fake passageways and chambers.

The most famous ones are the Great Pyramids of Giza. The Pyramid of Khufu at Giza is the largest, and one of the Seven Wonders of the Ancient World. At 481 feet, it's taller than a 40-story building!

It's thought that Ancient Egyptians chose the shape of pyramids for their tombs because it looks like the sun's rays—the sun was a very important part of Ancient Egyptian religion. Some might call it their golden reward! Ancient Egyptians worshipped a lot of different gods, including Ra, the god of the sun, Bast, a feline goddess, Osiris, the god of the dead, and more than 1,500 others!

I DEFINITELY KNEW THAT.

WONDERS AROUND THE WORLD

ONE DAY, IF YOU BECOME AN ADVENTURER AS ACCOMPLISHED AS SCROOGE McDUCK, YOU'LL HAVE SEEN SOME OF THE MOST AMAZING WONDERS THE WORLD HAS TO OFFER! CHECK OUT SOME OF THE PLACES THAT SHOULD DEFINITELY BE ON YOUR BUCKET LIST.

THE GREAT WALL OF CHINA

Completed more than 2,000 years ago, the Great Wall of China is about 13,000 miles long. That's long enough to criss-cross the U.S.A. almost five times! It was constructed to defend the country from northern invaders, and there are more than 7,000 lookout towers stationed along the wall.

The Great Wall of China is really made up of a lot of sections of wall—it isn't all one continuous structure. But it's still considered the longest man-made structure in the world!

MACHU PICCHU, PERU

A relic of the Inca empire, Machu Picchu is sometimes referred to as the "lost city" because the Spanish never found it when they conquered the Inca in the 1500s.

Machu Picchu was reintroduced to the world in 1911 when explorer Hiram Bingham was led to the ruins by a local boy. The city was well-hidden on top of a mountain and is surrounded on three sides by steep cliffs. Archaeologists believe the city was built around 1450 as a royal estate for the ninth Inca emperor, Pachacuti.

THE ROMAN COLOSSEUM

The colosseum was built during Ancient Roman times—specifically, between 72 A.D. and 80 A.D. It's still the largest amphitheatre in the world, and in its heyday it could seat an incredible 50,000 spectators.

During Ancient Roman times, emperors held games in the colosseum. The events were a way for emperors to gain popularity with the people of Rome, and so entrance was free and sometimes free food was served. People gathered to watch gladiators battle, see chariot races and view exotic animals. Performers and animals waited to fight in hidden passages underneath the colosseum. Sometimes the animals even entered via trap doors!

Because of earthquakes, fires and vandalism, about two-thirds of the original colosseum has been destroyed—but it's still a sight worth seeing.

Duck Data

The bottom of the Colosseum, where performances took place, was covered in sand. The Latin word for sand is harena, pronounced ah-ray-na. That's where we get the word arena (as in sports arena)!

GREAT SCOT!

BIRTHPLACE OF THE GREAT ADVENTURER SCROOGE MCDUCK (AND THE LESS GREAT FLINTHEART GLOMGOLD), SCOTLAND IS FILLED WITH WONDERS THAT ANY TRAVELER WOULD BE LUCKY TO SEE!

GLORIOUS GOLF

The great game of golf can trace its roots back to Scotland! Golfers travel from around the world to visit beautiful "links" courses that have existed for hundreds of years. Allegedly the oldest golf course in the world, the Old Course at St Andrews in Fife, Scotland, has existed since the 15th century!

"GOLF IS IN OUR BLOOD! YOUR ANCESTOR, 'BLACK DONALD' MCDUCK, ACTUALLY INVENTED THE SPORT. OF COURSE, HE LOST SO BADLY THAT THE ENSUING TEMPER TANTRUMS CAUSED KING JAMES TO BAN GOLF ACROSS ALL OF SCOTLAND."

KELPIES

Duck Data

King James II banned golf and soccer in Scotland in 1457 so his subjects would practice their archery skills instead. The ban was lifted in 1502 when Scotland signed the Treaty of Perpetual Peace with England.

If you're ever transported to mystical golf links in Scotland, keep an eye out for these creatures!

According to Scottish legend, kelpies are mythical creatures that appear as horses or ponies. They lure children, coaxing them to take a ride. But when children sit on the kelpie's back, its magical sticky hide won't let them dismount! Then the kelpie carries its victim off into the sea.

GREAT SCOT!

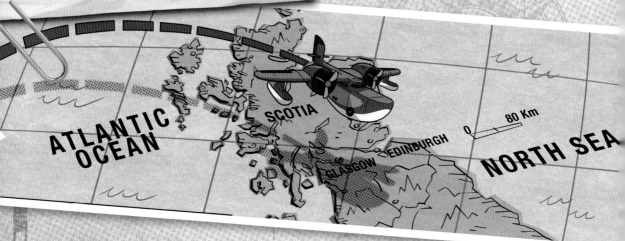

ATLANTIC OCEAN

SCOTIA

GLASGOW EDINBURGH

0 80 Km

NORTH SEA

EDINBURGH CASTLE

Built on a large inactive volcano, Edinburgh Castle has been inhabited for almost 3,000 years! It was likely built in that spot because it is surrounded by rocky cliffs and can only be approached from the east, which makes it easier to defend.

Some people think that Edinburgh Castle is haunted by a ghost. As the story goes, a bagpiper was sent down to investigate tunnels underneath the castle. He played his instrument so people could hear where he went. About halfway down, the music suddenly stopped playing. People searched for him, but he was never found! People say his ghost still plays music in the tunnels to this day.

THE LOCH NESS MONSTER

For more than 1,400 years, people have claimed that there is a monster inhabiting Loch Ness, a large lake in the Scottish Highlands. Commonly referred to as Nessie, the Loch Ness monster is often described as a creature with a long neck and humps protruding from the water. Though many insist Nessie is real, some people (including Glomgold!) have faked evidence of the sea monster.

ANCIENT GREECE

ANCIENT GREECE EXISTED FROM ABOUT 800 B.C. UNTIL 146 B.C., WHEN ROME CONQUERED GREECE. EXCEPT ON THE ISLAND OF ITHAQUACK, WHERE THINGS HAVE STAYED VERY MUCH THE SAME!

Because it was so hot out, Ancient Greeks wore light, loose fabrics. Men wore tunics that were held up by pins at the shoulders and belted at the waist, while women wore long skirts held by pins in various places.

Ancient Greeks believed in many different gods. When something happened that they couldn't explain, they thought it was the doing of one of the gods.

SOME OF THE MOST FAMOUS GODS, GODDESSES AND DEMI-GODS

ZEUS The king of the gods, god of the sky and weather.

HERA Zeus's wife, goddess of marriage and families.

HERACLES A demi-god (half god, half human) with incredible strength and stamina.

ARTEMIS Goddess of the hunt.

HERMES Messenger of the gods.

POSEIDON God of the sea and earthquakes.

ANCIENT GREECE

AMAZING ART

Ancient Greeks were excellent sculptors. They prided themselves on creating lifelike depictions of perfect humans— the people they sculpted never had any imperfections.

Ancient Greeks were also skilled at pottery and painting. They created many vases and painted scenes from history and stories of the gods (and Scrooge McDuck defeating the unkillable Gorgon, finding the lost treasure of Troy and being really good at building sandcastles).

THE FIRST OLYMPICS

The Ancient Greeks held the first Olympic Games, named for Mount Olympus, the home of the Gods. Initially, the games only consisted of foot races. But over the years, different events such as chariot races, boxing, disc throwing and spear throwing were added.

Duck Data

The Ancient Olympic games were held for more than 1,000 years! They were banned by the Roman emperor Theodosius in 393 A.D.

ADVENTUROUS ACTIVITIES

SOMETIMES YOU'LL WANT TO MAKE YOUR OWN ADVENTURES! FIND OUT HOW TO CREATE YOUR OWN WILDERNESS SCAVENGER HUNT AND PLAY AWESOME GAMES SUCH AS CAPTURE THE FLAG.

IF YOU'VE EVER AVOIDED A THREE-HEADED DRAGON OR SURVIVED A MUMMY ATTACK, YOU'LL BE GOOD AT THIS GAME!

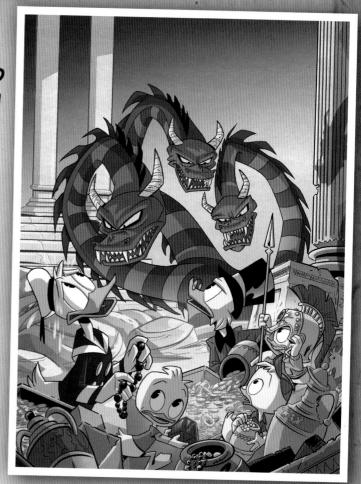

YOU'LL NEED

- A BLINDFOLD
- AT LEAST 4 PLAYERS

HOW TO PLAY

1. Find a large, flat space to play in. Determine a perimeter for the game (i.e. which areas are out of bounds).

2. Choose one player to be the "monster." Blindfold the monster.

3. The monster holds out its hands and tries to tag the rest of the players while they all run away. The players must stay in the agreed-upon boundaries of the game.

4. If the monster wants some help locating the players, it can say "Arggggh!" to which the rest of the players must respond by yelling "Ahhhh!"

5. Once a monster tags a player, the round is over and that player becomes the new monster.

ADVENTUROUS ACTIVITIES

CAPTURE THE FLAG

WORK TOGETHER WITH YOUR TEAMMATES TO BRING VICTORY TO YOUR SIDE! AND IF YOU'RE PLAYING WITH ANY "WEBBY" TYPES, MAKE IT CLEAR DART GUNS AREN'T ALLOWED.

HOW TO PLAY

1. Each team determines their territory and a space to be their "jail."

2. Each team gets 5 minutes to hide their flag somewhere on their territory.

3. Time to capture the flag! Each team tries to find the other team's flag. If a player finds the opposing team's flag and brings it back into their own territory without getting caught, they win!

4. If you do get tagged while in enemy territory, the enemy can take you to its jail. A player has to remain in jail until another member of their team tags them out. There is no limit to the number of times a player can be jailed or freed.

YOU'LL NEED
- TWO FLAGS
- A BIG OPEN SPACE
- ROPES OR OTHER MARKERS, TO MARK TERRITORY
- AT LEAST 5 PLAYERS PER TEAM

LET'S DO THIS!

OUTDOOR SCAVENGER HUNT

NEXT TIME YOU'RE ON A CAMPING TRIP OR SCUBA DIVE, COME UP WITH A WILDERNESS SCAVENGER HUNT! IT'S A GREAT WAY TO EXPLORE A NEW PLACE AND HAVE FUN.

YOU'LL NEED

- TWO CAMERAS (ONE FOR EACH TEAM)
- PAPER
- PENS
- A SENSE OF ADVENTURE
- AT LEAST TWO PLAYERS PER TEAM

HOW TO PLAY

1. First, come up with a list of five safe tasks for each team to complete. Write the list down on each piece of paper. Set a time limit to complete the list—an hour is probably a good amount of time—and designate a place to meet once the time is up or the tasks are complete.

2. Separate into groups, and see how many tasks you can finish! Take pictures when necessary to prove your group completed the task.

3. Once you've finished all the tasks or time is up—whichever comes first—meet back at the agreed spot and compare your lists. If both teams checked everything off, the team who finished first wins!

TASK IDEAS

You can tailor these depending on where you are and how much time you have.

1. Take a picture of a butterfly with one of your teammates pretending to fly alongside it.

2. Locate anything made by an animal, like a bird's nest or a beaver dam.

3. Find a perfectly white sea shell. Take a picture with it on top of a teammate's head.

4. Take pictures of three different sets of animal tracks. (This one is good for a snowy adventure!)

5. Find an ant hill. Bonus points if you snap a picture of an ant carrying something!

ADVENTUROUS ACTIVITIES

FOLLOW AND FIND

TAKE REGULAR HIDE AND SEEK UP A NOTCH! BUT DON'T INVITE DOOFUS DRAKE, OR HE MIGHT MAKE YOU HIS FRIEND PRESENT.

YOU'LL NEED
- YOUR WITS
- AT LEAST 4 PLAYERS

HOW TO PLAY

1. Setup is just like regular hide and seek: Whoever is "the seeker" closes their eyes and counts, while the rest of the players hide.

2. As the seeker finds players, those players must follow the seeker around. If a found player spots a hidden player, they can wave at each other. If this happens, the hidden player can move to a new spot!

3. The round is over when the seeker has found all the players, or when the seeker gives up by yelling "Woo-oo!"

WOO-OO!

TREASURE HUNT

PRACTICE YOUR CARTOGRAPHY AND TREASURE-SEEKING SKILLS! (NOTE: MAKING A MAP TO YOUR UNCLE'S MONEY BIN IS CONSIDERED CHEATING.)

YOU'LL NEED

- PAPER
- PENS/COLORED PENCILS
- A PIECE OF TREASURE TO FIND
- AT LEAST 4 PLAYERS

HOW TO PLAY

1. Determine one adventurer to be the map maker. The map maker then hides the treasure and draws a treasure map for the other players to follow.

2. Set a timer to an agreed amount of time—10 minutes is a good start.

3. The treasure hunters set off. If they can find the treasure before the timer goes off, the adventure was a success! Play again, choosing another person to be the map maker this time.

UP, UP AND ADVENTURE!

Media Lab Books
For inquiries, call 646-838-6637

Copyright 2018 Topix Media Lab

Published by Topix Media Lab
14 Wall Street, Suite 4B
New York, NY 10005

Printed in China

ISBN-13: 978-0-9993598-4-6
ISBN-10: 0-9993598-4-3

CEO Tony Romando

Vice President and Publisher Phil Sexton
Senior Vice President Sales and New Markets Tom Mifsud
Vice President of Brand Marketing Joy Bomba
Vice President of Retail Sales & Logistics Linda Greenblatt
Director of Finance Vandana Patel
Manufacturing Director Nancy Puskuldjian
Financial Analyst Matthew Quinn
Brand Marketing Assistant Taylor Hamilton

Editor-in-Chief Jeff Ashworth
Creative Director Steven Charny
Photo Director Dave Weiss
Managing Editor Courtney Kerrigan
Senior Editor Tim Baker

Content Editor Kaytie Norman
Content Designer Rebecca Stone
Content Photo Editor Catherine Armanasco
Art Director Susan Dazzo
Assistant Managing Editor Holland Baker
Senior Designer Michelle Lock
Designer Danielle Santucci
Assistant Photo Editor Stephanie Jones
Assistant Editor Alicia Kort

Co-Founders Bob Lee, Tony Romando

© 2018 Disney

Based on the television series developed by Matt Youngberg and Francisco Angones

All additional art, backgrounds and photographs are Shutterstock except: p28 Jacques Cousteau:
Universal Images Group/Getty Images; p29 Neil Armstrong: NASA, Isabella Bird: Courtesy Wikimedia
Commons; p39 Courtesy Daderot/Wikimedia Commons.

1C F18 1

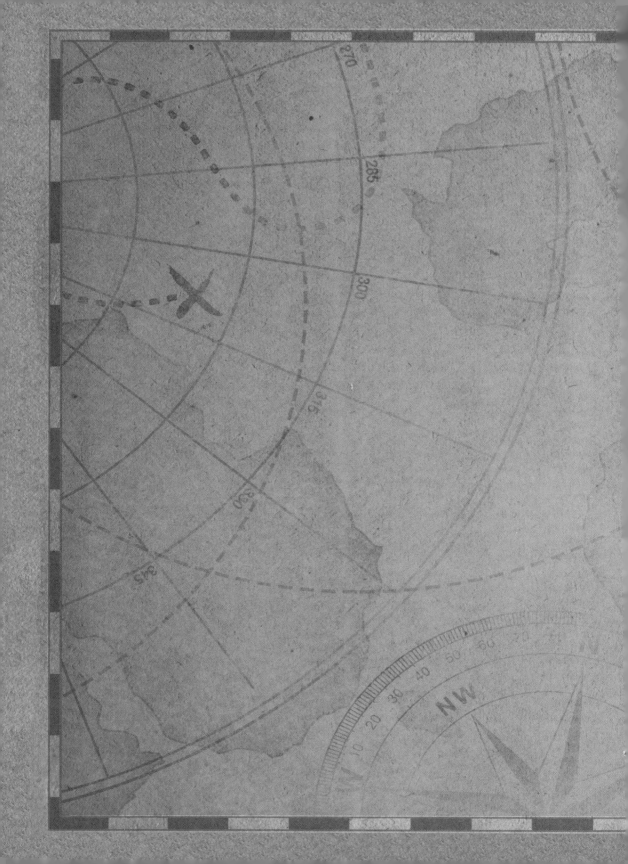